HYMNS
for Children

Elizabeth Laird
pictures by Margaret Tempest

COLLINS

For William

William Collins Sons & Co Ltd
London · Glasgow · Sydney · Auckland
Toronto · Johannesburg

© this collection Elizabeth Laird 1988
© illustrations the Estate of Margaret Tempest 1988

British Library Cataloguing in Publication Data

Laird, Elizabeth   Hymns for children.
   1. Christian church.   Public worship.   Hymns.
   Words – Anthologies – For children
   I. Title   II. Tempest, Margaret
   264′.2

ISBN 0-00-183172-0

Printed and bound in Belgium by Proost International Book Production

Foreword

The hymns in this book have been sung by generations of children. Some of them are very old: *Away in a manger* is from a hymn by Martin Luther; George Herbert wrote *Let all the world in every corner sing* in the seventeenth century; and Charles Wesley wrote *Gentle Jesus, meek and mild* in the eighteenth century.

The hymns we learn as children stay with us throughout our lives and their meaning becomes deeper and richer as time goes by. We hope that today's children will enjoy these hymns as much as their parents and grandparents did.

All people that on earth do dwell,
Sing to the Lord with cheerful voice;
Him serve with mirth, his praise forth tell,
Come ye before him and rejoice.

O enter then his gates with praise;
Approach with joy his courts unto;
Praise, laud and bless his name always,
For it is seemly so to do.

For why, the Lord our God is good:
His mercy is for ever sure;
His truth at all times firmly stood,
And shall from age to age endure.

To Father, Son and Holy Ghost,
The God whom heaven and earth adore,
From men and from the angel-host
Be praise and glory evermore.

William Kethe (died 1594)

All things bright and beautiful,
All creatures great and small,
All things wise and wonderful,
The Lord God made them all.

Each little flower that opens,
Each little bird that sings,
He made their glowing colours,
He made their tiny wings:

The tall trees in the greenwood,
The meadows where we play,
The rushes by the water
We gather every day:

He gave us eyes to see them,
And lips that we might tell
How great is God Almighty,
Who has made all things well:

Mrs Alexander (1818-1895)

Jesus, friend of little children,
Be a friend to me;
Take my hand and ever keep me
Close to thee.

Teach me how to grow in goodness,
Daily as I grow;
Thou has been a child, and surely,
Thou dost know.

Never leave me, nor forsake me,
Ever be my friend;
For I need thee from life's dawning
To its end.

Walter John Mathams (1853-1931)

Gentle Jesus, meek and mild,
Look upon a little child;
Pity my simplicity,
Suffer me to come to thee.

Lamb of God, I look to thee;
Thou shalt my example be:
Thou art gentle, meek and mild,
Thou wast once a little child.

Loving Jesus, gentle Lamb,
In thy gracious hands I am:
Make me, Saviour, what thou art;
Live thyself within my heart.

Charles Wesley (1707-1788)

Jesus, good above all other,
Gentle child of gentle mother,
In a stable born our brother,
Give us grace to persevere.

Jesus, who our sorrows bearest,
All our thoughts and hopes thou sharest,
Thou to man the truth declarest;
Help us all thy truth to hear.

Lord, in all our doings guide us;
Pride and hate shall ne'er divide us;
We'll go on with thee beside us,
And with joy we'll persevere.

Percy Dearmer (1867-1936)

Let all the world in every corner sing,
My God and King!
The heavens are not too high,
His praise may thither fly;
The earth is not too low,
His praises there may grow.
Let all the world in every corner sing,
My God and King!

Let all the world in every corner sing,
My God and King!
The Church with psalms must shout,
No door can keep them out;
But, above all, the heart
Must bear the longest part.
Let all the world in every corner sing,
My God and King!

George Herbert (1593-1633)

God make my life a little light
Within the world to glow;
A little flame that burneth bright,
Wherever I may go.

God make my life a little song
That comforteth the sad,
That helpeth others to be strong,
And makes the singer glad.

God make my life a little staff,
Whereon the weak may rest;
That so what health and strength I have
May serve my neighbour best.

Matilda Betham Edwards (1836-1919)

Loving Shepherd of thy sheep,
Keep thy lamb, in safety keep;
Nothing can thy power withstand,
None can pluck me from thy hand.

Loving Shepherd, ever near,
Teach thy lamb thy voice to hear;
Suffer not my steps to stray
From the strait and narrow way.

Where thou leadest I would go,
Walking in thy steps below,
Till before my Father's throne
I shall know as I am known.

Jane Eliza Leeson (1807-1882)

The wise may bring their learning,
The rich may bring their wealth,
And some may bring their greatness,
And some their strength and health:
We, too, would bring our treasures
To offer to the King;
We have no wealth or learning –
What shall we children bring?

We'll bring the many duties
We have to do each day;
We'll try our best to please him,
At home, at school, at play:
And better are these treasures
To offer to our King
Than richest gifts without them;
Yet these a child may bring.

Anon.

Away in a manger, no crib for a bed,
The little Lord Jesus laid down his sweet
  head,
The stars in the bright sky looked down
  where he lay –
The little Lord Jesus asleep on the hay.

The cattle are lowing, the baby awakes,
But little Lord Jesus, no crying he makes,
I love thee, Lord Jesus! Look down from
  the sky,
And stay by my side until morning is
  nigh.

Be near me, Lord Jesus; I ask thee to stay
Close by me for ever, and love me, I pray.
Bless all the dear children in thy tender
  care,
And fit us for heaven to live with thee
  there.

Martin Luther (1483-1546) trans. Anon.

Once in royal David's city
Stood a lowly cattle shed,
Where a mother laid her baby
In a manger for his bed:
Mary was that mother mild,
Jesus Christ her little child.

He came down to earth from heaven,
Who is God and Lord of all,
And his shelter was a stable,
And his cradle was a stall;
With the poor, and mean, and lowly,
Lived on earth our Saviour holy.

Mrs. Alexander (1818-1895)

Glory to thee, my God, this night
For all the blessings of the light;
Keep me, O keep me, King of kings,
Beneath thy own almighty wings.

Forgive me, Lord, for thy dear Son,
The ill that I this day have done,
That with the world, myself, and thee,
I, ere I sleep, at peace may be.

Praise God from whom all blessings flow;
Praise him, all creatures here below;
Praise him above, ye heavenly host;
Praise Father, Son, and Holy Ghost.

Bishop Ken (1637-1711)

All people that on earth do dwell

All things bright and beautiful

Fine

D.C.

Jesus, friend of little children

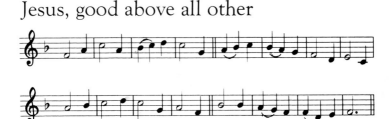

Gentle Jesus, meek and mild

Jesus, good above all other

Let all the world in every corner sing

God make my life a little light

Loving Shepherd of thy sheep

The wise may bring their learning

Away in a manger

Unison

Once in royal David's city

Glory to thee, my God, this night